for my friends
at the Saskatchewan School of the Arts

each summer

AUTHOR'S NOTE

This is only sort of a book, a not-quite-a-book book. It came into being as an accumulating heap of notes in a shoe box (hiking boots) in a filing cabinet. Or rather, it was the beginning of another book, a novel.

These journal entries were intended as reminders only. That they seldom stay on the subject indicates merely that when I was actually on the subject I proceeded with the writing of the novel, not with the keeping of a journal.

I see now, to my surprise, that almost five years elapsed between the writing of the first entry and the completion of the novel. Until I looked at these entries, I thought I'd written the novel in something of a hurry. Reminders are not always pleasant.

But to be reminded of friends is genuinely and always a pleasure. To the many friends whose names appear in this journal, I have only one apology to offer: I'd have made fuller notes, added much illuminating commentary and analysis, had I known I was writing this book, and not another one.

Robert Kroetsch

INTRODUCTION

The writer writing
catching himself in the act of
catching himself in the act of
what   exactly   yes   what
The term "journal" can refer to anything from the detailed daily
accounts of life & art, of people seen & work accomplished, found in
Le Journal des Goncourt or the *Diaries* of Virginia Woolf to the
commonplace books kept by a writer like Auden. The form is
always self-reflexive: intensely so in the case of the Brothers
Goncourt or Woolf; apparently not, or almost not, in the case of
Auden. Nevertheless, even Auden's quotations, insofar as they
speak directly to his feelings & interests, & thus reflect his sense of
self, become his "own" statements, part of *his* journal. Writers
write; & many of them write a great deal beyond the narrow
confines of their published *oeuvre*. Not just failed or poor works,
but notes, in various forms, to themselves about...well, about just
about everything. Some write letters, for example, in which they
continually manage to carry on two dialogues: one with whomever
they're writing to this time; the other, central, one with themselves,
arguing once more their obsessions, their needs, their desperate
efforts to say what they have, to say. I suspect that if we ever get a
Kroetsch *Letters* (& I for one look forward to it), we'll find he
continually speaks to his own, & others', efforts as Canadian,
prairie, artists, as well as to the immediate concerns of his
correspondents.

As a "journalist," Kroetsch falls somewhere between the
compulsive daily scribbler & the cool, distanced copier. His
"notes," on scattered bits of paper which then find their way into "a
shoebox (hiking boots) in a filing cabinet," are dated: they are like
diary entries, except for the feel of the accidental attached to them,
& the fact that they are in no way "daily." So he is a kind of diarist.
But they often mention what he's reading & reflect upon that. So he
is sometimes like a copier. But instead of copying out what he reads,
Kroetsch usually comments upon it: knowing the book will be there
to reread when he wants to, all he wants now is to *note* his
engagement with whatever has touched him. So he's just another
occasional note-maker. Thus these "journal entries" are somewhat
haphazard, the product not of a deliberate & disciplined attempt to
record his own life but rather of a catch-as-catch-can process,

written only when he remembered to, or, perhaps more importantly, *felt the need to* say something about events & situations in his life.

Though not a long book, *The Crow Journals* covers five years from the first conception of *What the Crow Said* to its publication. Thus the many hiatuses, of weeks & even months, between entries are significant. They speak of two different kinds of experiences: 1) the mundane, everyday living Kroetsch felt no need to record & 2) the actual *writing* of his novels & poems, during which he had no time to notice, or at least *note*, whatever else might be happening around him. That *The Crow Journals* is nevertheless an entertaining, fascinating & lively series of glimpses into the concommitant processes of living & writing, of living writing, is due to the fact that Kroetsch is a writer of great charm & wit who always thinks himself into whatever he writes as fully as possible, even a journal entry intended only as a reminder of something or other for himself.

Like so many of Kroetsch's fictions, *The Crow Journals* is a kind of quest, in a kind of labyrinth, & it continually conjugates beginnings & endings. Neither exists fully separate from the other except perhaps in birth & death, & Kroetsch has always been fictionally fascinated by their varied & various conjunctions. But in the very act of putting these "notes" in order, of making a book out of them & therefore choosing to have *a* beginning & *an* ending, Kroetsch also dis/covers a form in which a pattern of intermingled beginnings & endings, endings & beginnings, becomes meaningfull.

The quests here are fairly clear. The major one is the lengthy search for the novel in its finished form. Yet it begins, or he begins to imagine it, before he has finished the final draft of *Badlands*. He also begins & finished other works — poems & poem sequences, some books of poems — during the writing of *What the Crow Said*, & begins his latest book, *The Sad Phoenician*, before the journal ends. The writing life, so long as the writing is a focal part of the living, is a continual series of beginnings, & their concomitant endings. The search, for something more or else to say, is lifelong, never ending.

The writing life is also the writer's life, & here too Kroetsch discovers a number of emotional beginnings & endings, endings with new beginnings implicit in them. Here the image of the labyrinth provides a useful analogue for the *Journals'* crazy quilt of journeys crisscrossing each other through space (& time). Within the arbitrary limits of the published journal, they begin & end in Binghamton. That city is the entrance to a labyrinth whose centre, paradoxically & only in terms of these notes as object/book, is the prairies, especially Fort San, the home of the Saskatchewan School of the Arts where Kroetsch visited each summer from 1974 to 1977. From that center, Kroetsch finally retraces his steps to Binghamton, where the final entry finds him: getting ready to leave, for good, to shift the whole labyrinth to a new location. Yet even the final leave-taking is the beginning of a return: he will go back & forward to the home/space he's never left in his writing & continually visited in his life: a kind of exile's return except he was never the usual exile anyway. Writer & man, man most clearly defined as writer, Kroetsch moves through a series of changes, of comings & goings (beginnings & endings), & takes notes along the way which both entertain his readers & help us, along with him, to perceive the important questions confronting a writer in his place today.

These questions, parts of his quest as a writer, arise out of his many engagements with others & with the tradition in his guises as writer, editor, teacher &, centrally, generous friend. Moreover, perhaps the most important questions are the ones he never answers except (perhaps) implicitly in the work. For the artist, after all, questions or problems remain to be explored over & over again. *A* solution is not *the* solution: one continues to write because the large questions continue to demand responses (though perhaps not final answers).

A number of almost narrative paths weave through the maze-like structure of the *Journals*. There is the writing of the novel, the series of references to aspects of the book or to what he has accomplished so far. Attached to these notes are the various references to Gabriel Garcia Marquez's great fiction, *One Hundred Years of Solitude*, a novel which obviously influenced Kroetsch in his dis/covery of what was, for him, an essentially new narrative method after his exhaustion of one kind of self-conscious writing in the novels from *The Studhorse Man* through *Badlands*. Winding in & out around this central path are those concerned with his life & thinking as a teacher of modern & post-modern literature & as an editor of *boundary 2*, a journal of post-modern literature. In these notes, Kroetsch stubbornly & insistently argues himself out of & in to literature as it is & can be, the possibiities of language & narrative, the need to tell stories & the importance of writing poems. As he edits the special Canadian issue of *boundary 2*, he typically piles some creative poetics on the need to break forms & some marvelously generous responses to other writers — "those Vancouver poets who dare everything" — into one short surge of vital speech. Meanwhile his notes keep slipping among the forms, refusing to stay fact or fiction, prose or poetry, but rather insisting in their transformations that living speech is all those things & more. And why not.

If the writer-editor-teacher speaks & seeks his way through one part of this labyrinth of time, the friend & lover also seeks *his* path. Kroetsch goes to conferences, to readings, to Fort San, to Calgary, Lethbridge & Winnipeg as Writer-in-Residence. Or he welcomes people to whatever resting-place he's found for a particular nonce. His interactions with people — lovers, friends, fellow-writers, students — enter the *Journal* because in them too he confronts aspects of the writing life, the problems he sees as central to anyone trying to tell the stories of "our" land: the prairies, Canada. So his comments on Rudy Wiebe for example, or on the young writers he meets at Fort San & Winnipeg, are generous but also subtly aware of the significance of their efforts & the incredible difficulties they & he face.

Kroetsch the writer & Kroetsch the teacher are inextricably a part of each other. There are few Canadian writers who pay such *conscious* attention to what they are about. Many of these notes concern new discoveries he makes while he works his way through the first draft of *What the Crow Said*, for his kind of self-awareness & discipline does not include planning everything ahead of time as an Arthur Hailey would but rather a studied readiness to uncover previously unglimpsed possibilities in the exploration his writing is for him & follow them through. But this is only the beginning, as his entry for May 4, 1976 reveals: he has finally finished his first draft so the novel exists; but he's only finished the first draft so the novel still has to be written. The literary endeavour is to create a palimpsest of sufficiently complex depths it can hold all writer & reader bring to it. In fact not only will he rewrite in order to deepen & strenghten the language of the story but he will continue to dis/cover new pieces of the puzzle he didn't even know was still unfinished; & the notes display such moments of discovery occurring. As we read we see it happening & perhaps begin to comprehend both how & why it does. Indeed, it's only as he begins to *re*write, that he begins to make a number of fascinating paradoxical statements about his relation to tradition, convention & the new work he's engaged on. The questions & the quest to "make it new" arise, as they should, from his re/vision of the work he's trying to shape fully now.

Nevertheless, though *The Crow Journals* is first & foremost a journal of the writing of *What the Crow Said* (& note how late & in what delightful fashion Kroetsch realizes his title), it is also a journal of journeys through space & time with other people. Kroetsch, the master story-teller *in print*, an A-1 Hard Northern bullshitter who nevertheless doesn't "tell" stories except when he writes them down (so he tells us), doesn't so much tell the stories of the people & parties he encounters along the way as he alludes to them. Writing about a party in Winnipeg where Al Purdy & W. O. Mitchell competed in "a wonderful lying contest," Kroetsch realizes the *story* of the party & the confrontation mostly by implication. The reason, of course, is that Kroetsch is writing for himself at this point rather than an audience. But because he is a committed writer, he makes even such notes lively & energetic forays into language. So time & again he gives capsule descriptions of people he meets which vividly & idiosyncratically realize their uniqueness as human beings in his vision. Rather than adjectival, physical description, he attempts an active articulation of their perceived selves as they engage him or their writing. Kroetsch is, as I have already intimated, an incredibly generous man but he doesn't lack standards. One of his students at Fort San has suggested that it's precisely his generosity of spirit towards young writers which demands immense efforts on their parts. At the same time, it becomes obvious that other writers form a community to which Kroetsch gives his heartfelt commitment. That sense of community shines through in the pages on Fort San, the visits with Rudy Wiebe or to the West Coast, & it is important.

Always intelligently questioning the world, Kroetsch also always seeks the right words. The varied forms of humour in the *Journal* are but one testament to this search. Kroetsch loves good wit & good jokes, especially when they inhere in the spoken language. A typical example of his humour & his style in action is his description of bookseller William Hoffer. Dinner with a number of West Coast writers in Nanaimo elicits an equally compelling though not specifically comic response. A *Journal* like this allows us to watch a writer noticing what goes on about & within him. Kroetsch notices & notes: his articulation of his perceptions & speculations provides us with insights into the writing life of one writer; those insights also provoke us to speculate about the whole situation of the artist in Canada today.

Robert Kroetsch is now living in Calgary. Since this *Journal* ended, he has passed through more beginnings & endings. From Manitoba he has come all the way back to Alberta. He has completed *The Sad Phoenician* & seen it published & has begun new projects. One of them is the publication of *The Crow Journals*. But surely this only whets the appetite for more: more of his journals from before & after the period covered in this book, as well as a *Collected Letters* someday. As one of the most interesting theorists of post-modern writing in Canada, he has much to tell us; as a charming & witty writer he can be depended upon to entertain us. This is the writing of a lively, active, wise (& foolish), comic visionary. Enjoy it.

Douglas Barbour
University of Alberta
November 1979

THE *CROW* JOURNALS

Sunday, November 25, 1973
Binghamton, New York

Recovering from the flu. Home and in bed for a week. Reading *Under the Volcano* while in a kind of delirium. Fever and ideas. That old vice, writing titles:

Winter Work (on writing/Canadian)

Rocky Mountain Year (a year in the Rockies)

novel: HOME/PARKLANDS/COUSINS — dishonest, idealistic, drinking (Bob Edwards?) printer — itinerant prairie printer, as center, as ultimate story center/teller: my own (rural?) experience, basically, expanded towards the tall tale, the mythological; but always the hard core of detail.

PRINTER'S DEVIL — a member of the family who goes to work for the printer. " _____ printer needed money." Opening. He decides to put together a history of the town of ; the family of; slowly becomes involved,

unearths weird episodes, hidden characters and motives; slowly begins to put together a mythic/epic/comic/telltale of the family/town/west of this version of man.

Friday, December 14, 1973
Binghamton, New York

...Yesterday, in class at 9 a.m., a student giving a report on Lowry insisted that we had to sample tequila in order to understand his report on *Volcano* and vision. He produced, as if by magic, from under the table, a bottle of tequila. We went from his report to an early lunch in the campus pub. Beer and talk of writing. Two of the students, one a motorcycle fanatic, both Olson fanatics come here from the U of Connecticut, insisted on a "right reading" of *The Maximus Poems*. Loud protests and more pitchers of beer and passers-by joining our table....Then to my office to meet briefly with, advise, a blind student, a folk-singer. Saw L at work in her office, grading papers. She and I went to the pub, met more friends and went to Sharkey's for a supper of spiedies and steamed clams. Lost one of her contact lens, in my car. The absurd search (we found it) leading to our second meeting, today...

Tuesday, December 18, 1973
Binghamton, New York

even then,
unsatisfied

for whatever, in the first
the (necessary) descent

then the parklands, the home, the sacred place
the undying of the hero

and after, the goatish
reversal, the tragic
joke.

How I must always shape this whole labyrinth of the world. A novel into language. Trying to begin again, I invent my theory of the uninvention of the world, then plot anew. Beginning to see what I must do to rewrite *Badlands*. Beginning to see what is not quite. The farther shaping against the central notes. How to circumference the moving point....

Thursday, December 20, 1973
Binghamton, New York

Pat Batten teased me because I keep my pocket watch in a bottom drawer of my desk while I'm in my office, writing. I claim it makes too much noise. She claims that I want to keep time boxed up, enclosed.

Tuesday, January 1, 1974
Binghamton, New York

Last night, no midnight party. For the first time in many years. Instead, talked with my wife, agreed that her lawyer is right, that she is right. Separation. Endings before beginnings.

Just back from the meeting of the Modern Languages Association in Chicago. Interviewed job candidates mostly. Realized I don't need to go to new places at the moment. I don't want to. Rather, I want to go back to the old, to see how time worked. The prairie novel as a time novel now. Time itself doing the (un)structuring.

I have been to the water's edge,
and heard the water's story.

Each day, a borrowing
against the night.

And love's only portal, too.

Tuesday, January 22, 1974
Binghamton, New York

Went skating yesterday. Took Meg to the auditorium, where the Broome Dusters play hockey. Laura recovering from a cold. The lost pleasure recalled, skating on sloughs, or on the Battle River. And the time my mother fell, while she was skating, teaching me to skate; the slough across the road from our farmhouse frozen before the first snow, a half-mile sheet of ice; my mother using her coat as a sail. And falling. My fear.

Dropping cutlery.
"Going to have visitors."
  fork — woman
  spoon — bachelor
  knife — man

Remember taking Laura to the Ross Park Zoo to ride on the carousel, to ride on those painted horses, those horses that gallop, even when they stand still. From a distance, approaching the carousel, pausing at the bear cage, we heard the music from the carousel. "Daddy," Laura said, "the horses are singing."

Monday, January 28, 1974
Manhattan, New York

The Hudson River outside, the river below the window. New Jersey over there. And up the river the George Washington Bridge, the convexity of steel.

A whole unlearning of the acquired self, back to the boy who would have written the novel. To letting him write it.

In a friend's apartment, to have lunch. When she turns on the kitchen light the cockroaches scatter into hiding. The dining room, elegant and precise. We spread linen napkins on our laps. The gulls below us, skimming the water. A tugboat heading upriver.

Wednesday, February 27, 1974
Binghamton, New York

Reading William Carlos Williams again. *Kora in Hell.* *Spring and All.* Pointing me to where I'm at. Not Olson. No, no, not Olson. Olson lacking a heart in some sad way, lacking a way to let in the variety, the plainness, the extravagance. But Williams is there all the time: taking the risks. Moving from poetry to prose to poetry.

Thursday, February 28, 1974
Binghamton, New York

Breaking forms. Today I'm editing Warren Tallman's essay on Vancouver poetry of the 60s for *boundary 2.* I end up wanting to break the form of the journal itself. It becomes so goddamned *orderly* as we edit. Tallman's inability to spell is part of the freedom of his essay. Along with his sense of where mountain and energy meet. Bowering. Kiyooka. Marlatt. Wah. And his recognition of the cold rage of Davey, the complexity of Hindmarch's insistence on simplicity. The geography of museness. I'll put into the issue — pictures of crashing airplanes. Against a humanism that coerces. Those Vancouver poets who dare everything.

Saturday, March 9, 1974
Binghamton, New York

Last night, or this morning at 1 p.m., Sheila phoned from Petaluma, California. Lee had a heart attack in the Santa Rosa airport, was dead upon arrival in the hospital. I was stunned, confused, half asleep, unable to give the sympathy that she expected of me. And in bed, alone, after, I remembered the death of my mother. I remembered the wake, the crowds of people arriving over muddy roads, the body in the coffin in my parents' bedroom. And I remembered the men who came to my father and tried to tell him of the sorrow they felt: and even at the age of 13 I saw the failure of language, the faltering connection between those spoken words and what it was I knew my father felt, what I felt...Fell asleep, finally, and had a nightmare. I was in a dimly lit bedroom. My Aunt Annie came into the room, sat down on the floor, because she wanted to talk to me. And at times in our lives she did tell me things, for I would listen to her tales of family history. She was unable to read or write and had instead a memory that covered many decades. I was not wise enough to listen carefully or to write down what she had to say, and now it's lost...But back to the dream. She sat down on the floor, old, small, and I bent over to hear her. And as I bent over someone, something, behind me, threw a stifling quilt over me from behind, closed it around me, down over my head. I woke up crying out loud and in dread.

Friday, March 15, 1974
Flying over Saskatchewan

Twelve hours after the worst blizzard in recent years. The snowplow operators on strike. The prairies an unmarked blanket of snow....Many years past...three feet of snow with absolutely no wind...the buffalo starved because the wind didn't sweep the grass clear....Flying to Lethbridge via Chicago and Winnipeg and Calgary. To talk to geographers. Then on to San Francisco.

The weight of recurrence versus what happens uniquely, for the first time, now. Love. Or love.

   My wife as she drove me to the airport: "You have your own clock."
"What does that mean?"
"It prevents union."
"Can I be otherwise?"
"Some of it is willed. Some of it is natural."

The loss of identity that begins so quickly, while one waits in an airport.

Tuesday, March 26, 1974
Binghamton, New York

Working on the Canadian issue of *boundary 2* yesterday. The genius of place, of that new old place, must be located in the literature itself, not in the absent gods.

Recalled, last night, going out on a loaded barge in darkness on the Mackenzie River. The narrow walkway between the heaped freight and the rushing water. The fear. And the pleasure too. In the danger. A version of terror. A poem about it. The process of naming can be a process of defusing. Language: a retreat from the demonized.

In Canada: do we have polis? Has the Canadian city been invented? Or are the rural values still dominant, and with those values the stories, the memories, that carry them? Again that novel I should write: *The Gates of the City.* The change that does, must, take place at the moment of entry.

Friday, May 3, 1974
Binghamton, New York

She tells me: I give too much attention to the profane over the sacred. Perhaps I do. But in the profane I hear, find, the sacred. Without the one there cannot be the other. The necessary love quarrel.

This morning in L's apartment. The profane surprise of her body, when she undresses.

John Barth visiting campus today. His saying about Marquez what I recognized, felt in my blood — that he, Marquez, is at the center of postmodern in this last half of the 20th century. The coming down from high art while including it. The young Puerto Rican graduate student on whose final oral I was outside reader: his saying, My mother understood *One Hundred Years of Solitude* and wept....Barth very attractive, master of the professorial attitude and writer too, guardian of the language, gentle, wise, willing to put himself down...

Tuesday, May 14, 1974
Binghamton, New York

now celebrate life
now celebrate death
and love all the companee

Last Saturday: the English Graduate Organization picnic. A glorious day, playing softball (hit a three-bagger), eating chicken, drinking keg beer. After the picnic L and I drove out to the edge of the Catskills.

Yesterday: refused to pass a dissertation on John Hawkes. The central chapter not yet there....Symbolism may have spent its force, in its present form. But realism is not the answer. Rather a new version of the fabulist....My reading Hawkes, rereading.

Friday, May 17, 1974
Binghamton, New York

Finished grading papers yesterday. Now, possibly, again, the writer. The son remembering the story-telling father. Uncle Paul and his stories. One of the reasons why I'm a novelist, I suppose.

We weave and unweave ourselves. The good person, gentle, kind, wise, considerate, a father and husband, a man who needs a wife, children, home. And then the son of a bitch who can't stand those things, the stud, the charlatan, the bastard, the wild drinking man, the deceiver and liar, the tall-tale self....Maybe. I don't know. But I do know something about Yeats and his opposing selves, and I do know that the risk of creation involves the risk of destruction.

The new novel stirring in my imagination again this morning. A man who has nineteen daughters who each and all get knocked up, one by one....But I still have *Badlands* to complete. And poems, working in my head. And an invitation from the U of Lethbridge, to spend a year there as writer-in-residence. Must think about what it means: that time, that prairie-lit place. And the isolation too.

To invent: a character who knows more, has done more, than the author.

Thursday, May 30, 1974
Binghamton, New York

My arguing, yesterday, today, again, that only sex and drinking and writing matter, and she, her smile exciting, her strong, slightly flawed teeth exciting; while we made love I was writing poems, landscape flowing through my mind, some sandhills in Manitoba, the badlands of the Red Deer, a lake on the edge of North Bay: her body and the world: two chapters to work on in *Badlands*, the departure out of Deadlodge Canyon. The new novel to torment me: the hero, Liebhaber. That stubborn naming. The lover. The amateur. L going away for the week end, taking with her Marquez to read. As exciting to me as Faulkner was, those many years ago. Without the intrusion of Faulknerian language. Marquez, translated, lets me get at the story, the characters, the paragraphs, the place of time, the stretching time of place...

Wednesday, June 5, 1974
Binghamton, New York

And so we come to exile, finally. As if I sought it out and only last night found it. After years without quite having a country. Now, separating from wife and children, I have the sense of being totally without place. Not even a place to take friends for a drink when, yesterday, in the middle of rewriting *Badlands*, I had the realization that it's finished. I stopped, took 30 pages to a typist in the Library Tower for retyping. L and I joined two graduate students who are washing windows for the summer, and we went to The Ale House.

In *Modern Fiction Studies*, Spring 73. Page 107: a footnote to an essay on Gass's "In the Heart of the Heart of the Country." Paul Zweig: "The adventurer is in flight from women. Because he cannot cope with the erotic and social hegemony of women, he flees them even into death." And he locates the pattern in medieval romance. And thus too the pattern in *The Studhorse Man*. The posture of the hero demanding of him the quest-flight. The fear of domesticity, of community.

Today. Towards a new novel? The figure of Liebhaber? Last night I dreamt of the little town of Rosalind. It was, instead of its scattered self in the midst of farms, a perfected town hidden away in the wilds of Alberta. I went to visit, to see my aunt, my cousins (the McDonalds). As I drove into town a stream at its edge was rising. Then a huge flood....When I was a boy, my Aunt Margaret's garden was a source of wonder. One of the versions of Eden.

Sunday, July 7, 1974
Qu'Appelle Valley Saskatchewan

Flew to Regina today. Bus to Fort Qu'Appelle. A ride out to Fort San, to the cluster of handsome old buildings and lawns and trees that used to be a TB sanitarium. Now: a summer school of the arts. Here in a long, deep coulee of the Qu'Appelle Valley, facing onto Echo Lake. Music, as if the birds themselves have taken up the clarinet. Dance. Young girls, proud in their new bodies. Photography. Writing.

I'm to be visiting writer at the writers' conference for a couple of weeks. I arrived early and unannounced. Found the writers' lounge in a plain, comfortable wooden dormitory hidden away behind the central brick buildings. I went into the lounge to pick up sheets and a towel and was told, immediately, of a strange writer who'd arrived from Ontario, stayed one hour, and left. I made my way to my monk-like room on the second floor. A cot. A chair. A combination dresser-desk. I hung up the sports jackets that I have, ridiculously, brought along. Hung a shirt over the mirror so I can work without seeing myself. Went to sign for a typewriter. Ended up walking down to the beach with an intense young girl who, abruptly, told me of the young man who dropped her off early — as the final act of their relationship. She wanted to cry but couldn't. Or wouldn't. I threw stones at the water, trying to make them skip. We sat on a water-worn log, the dry-eyed girl and I, looking out across the lake at the far shore.

Escapes and separations and abandonment.
People without names.
What is this?

Sunday, July 14, 1974
Qu'Appelle Valley, Saskatchewan

Ken Mitchell in charge; Ken a complicted, wild, generous, easy-going, intense man...contradictory, driven...moving away from fiction, towards drama, it seems to me...as a way to working with his contradictions.

This arts center, on the sloping ground facing the lake...a kind of theater. With theaters within. And my god the talent. Lorna Uher, a poet of wild energy, directing all of us into nightly rituals of joy. Last night: the beer parlor in Lebret. Talking, talking. All of us. And at once. Mrs. Mitchell there too, an intense and profoundly aware woman who brilliantly complements Ken's personality. In her own refusal of "personality."

Reg Silvester. In the room next to mine. A young prose writer, hesitating to explore the labyrinth of his own imagination. Byrna Barclay. Entered into the labyrinth. Acting on a clue given by a Metis friend, she is entered into a vision of exile and return.

I was sitting outside the old wooden schoolhouse, up on the hill behind this dormitory, making notes to myself. That first half of a novel that is all scratches and guesses. Mostly I was enjoying the sun. And watching a young woman who was also sitting in the sun, writing. She was writing, rapidly, and I watched her gestures, her patterns of concentration. Hot sun. Grasshoppers, making the sound of that prairie light. Caraganas, letting down their green shadows against the heat. Light and shadows and that woman enjoying so much the sun, her long hair loose and dark, her right arm, pale, moving. I didn't yet know her name. But I had a glimpse, in that one hour, of the opening of my novel, the novel's shape. That woman, writing her story, unwittingly writing mine.

We went for a walk, she and I, before supper. She was educated in a convent. She is a farmer's wife. She is active in the environmental movement and wants to write in its service.

Wednesday, August 21,1974
Binghamton, New York

Bill Spanos back today from his year in France and Greece. Hurray. We went to the pub at 3:30, drank and ate pizza until six. People coming in to welcome Bill. To hear his reports on the political situation in Greece. His hair-breadth escape: he's of Greek descent and by law subject to the draft....Spanos, while serving in the American army, was taken prisoner by the Germans, was a POW in Dresden and worked at the task of picking up bodies after the fire-bombing. Later escaped and wandered behind lines....All part of what made him an existentialist....The Greek colonels, threatening him again. Spanos and his commitment to Heidegger, to *Dasein*. Being-in-the-world. There-being....Even while we bitch about the endless task of editing *boundary 2*, the endless hassle to find money...we begin to plan a Heidegger issue.

A letter, yesterday, from Ken Mitchell in Saskatchewan. Inviting me back to the arts center next year....The experience was a profound one, the communal life, and the landscape itself, the people at-home in the landscape. *Dasein*. The figure of Tiddy, in my novel. Theodora. Gift of God. But always in the world. Tiddy Lang.

Thursday, August 22, 1974
Binghamton, New York

Imaginative possession of place, not material possession.

With Meg and Laura, driving out to Matt Corrigan's house in the country. He's away on vacation. Corrigan, a brilliant young phenomenologist, fascinated by Lowry and Olson, those two "ruined" great writers — Corrigan, a student of the phenomenology of failure that makes for what others might call success, living alone in this early 19th century house. Tending his garden. Reading. I'm looking after his house while he's away. I walk to the stream behind his house, cross over the stream and walk into the small cornfield beyond. Small fields along the bottom of the valley, surrounded by maple and oak and all the trees of the hardwood forest. The eastern forest that remains always a mystery to me. An old graveyard up the road a few yards from Matt's house. It draws the visitors who come to the house, they go walk in the graveyard.

Driving out with Meg and Laura. Meg and Laura talking about the animals you can and can't eat. Laura wondered what a human tastes like. Meg (age 8) said, "If you eat a person you eat his soul." Laura and I fell silent. I saw, in the mirror, a smile come over Meg's face. "Sometimes, daddy," she said, "I don't understand what I say."

The history of the future. Must use that.

Friday, August 30, 1974
Binghamton, New York

Lunch in The Pub with L and the poet Bob Pawlikowski and the painter David Shapiro and the sculptor Jim Stark. Wild comic/serious discussion of the need to learn to be naive. What I would call the postmodern impulse (one dimension of it). Can you learn your way back to naivete? No. Yes, but no. David's story of the man who painted a picture of Warhol by holding magic markers in his asshole.

I remember one time, as a kid, trying to screw a large stone. A boulder left by the retreating glaciers, I suppose. I was walking across the fields east from our house to where the O'Connors lived at the time. Even then, alone, I knew I was attempting something strange, ridiculous, incomprehensible, necessary. Became aroused. Tried to screw the stone.

L retreating from the conversation, withdrawing from me. We mentioned Eliade. She somehow can't endure "abstract" talk. But myth isn't abstract to me. Like trying to screw that stone.

Saturday, September 14, 1974
Binghamton, New York

No charge in the language. No energy. Trying to write this morning, and I couldn't make it come alive on the level of language itself. L and I went to Valley Offset, Deposit, to read *"blues"* for an issue of *boundary 2*, then kept going. Up into the mountains. Wild storm in the Catskills, lightning, rain, a tree falling near the bar. Got high in a bar down by the Beaverkill, west of Roscoe....One time, Dave Carpenter, visiting here from Alberta, drove with me into the Catskills, showed me a poisonous snake, told me the history of all these famous trout streams that he'd never seen but knows so much about. I, living here, now knowing. Language itself, the trickster, perhaps.

Sunday, September 15, 1974
Binghamton, New York

To work at eight, in my new, secret office in Hinman College. Trying to keep books *out* of this office. The walls a stark white. A desk. One set of shelves. A filing cabinet. Four bright blue chairs. Should get my most recently acquired Eskimo print (two fish, blue) framed and hung in here on a white wall. Should get some of those little gourds....A draft of an opening. Another draft of another opening. "That was the spring the snow didn't melt...." Beautiful, sunny day. So at noon we went for lunch, L and I, then for a drive. To Rock Road. Up the hillside we found an old (forestry?) road, almost vanished into the forest, then found a meadow, then, without quite intending to (the sun was just there, just shining, the sky clear), found ourselves in the sun, in the grass, making love. Three horsemen went by, up the trail, but somehow didn't notice us. Or at least, pretended not to.

Wednesday November 20, 1974
Binghamton, New York

Last night, read again William Gass's *In the Heart of the Heart of the Country*. He calls us to the forgotten compulsion: the need not only to write, but to write absolutely....His ability to make story out of smalltown civilization; his ability to make poetry out of the language of that civilization.

Work and love. Work and love. Freud or someone. The curse of my life: women who have love, but no equal work.

Things can't be as bad as they are.

Inside the pumpkin   I feel much better.

My honors course: The Possibilities of the Novel. Should have been: Postmodern Man on His Last Legs. Took on the course when a medievalist who wanted to do some work in modern suddenly became an administrator. Six gifted students. The pleasure of teaching, the immediate satisfaction. The temptation to forget about the writing that takes years of silence.

Saturday, December 21, 1974
Binghamton, New York

The possible no long interests me. A thought for the first day of winter.

Remembering absurdities. Like when Little Joe was killed on a barge at Norman Wells. Two of us going from the bow of the barge to the manhole where he was caught in flame. And I tried to speak and my mouth was full of the chocolate cake I'd been eating when we heard the boom. The whoosh of flame. Joe's skin falling off as he kept on crawling up the ladder, his hair burnt off, his clothes gone, except for his belt and his boots and his jockey shorts. Joe dead and still climbing, talking.

Took my daughters to a tree farm. To cut a Christmas tree.

Wednesday, January 1, 1975
Manhattan, New York

Yesterday, two days ago, L and I in the Rand McNally store on 53rd St., looking at maps. Two of North America — 1650, 1700 — with Western Canada blank. My imagination, fired out of all season by those blank spaces.

books, The Eighth Street Bookshop,
yesterday: Ponge
          Blackburn
          a book on back-packing
          essays on Kierkegaard   12.80

Strand Book Store, 828 Broadway:
          second-hand books on
          Japanese prints   3.78

The Metropolitan Museum of Art
to see: *The Duke of Berry*
          Book of Hours   1.50

Not the map itself, but the blank spaces.

New Year's Eve. L and I in Chapman's Restaurant on 53rd. Drinking a lot. After dining in a Japanese restaurant. After the ballet, "Coppelia" and the newly arrived sensation of Baryshnikov. Thinking: Natalia Makarova, not Baryshnikov, was the real reason for seeing "Coppelia." I preferred the Eliot Feld Ballet production, "Embrace the Tiger and Return to Mountain." Saw it Dec 27. Straight out venture into new structure. Using a system of shadow boxing developed in China in the 6th century. Postmodern.

Rain, rain, rain falling. Horns and hats. Went back to our hotel singing in the streets, others singing, blowing horns. A new year/

Wednesday, June 4, 1975
Binghamton, New York

Marquez — has cracked the problem of how to tell a story in third
person again. Voice: a calm distancing that enables him to forget
the conventions of realism. The effect of a story in translation, as in
Melquiades' case.

Saturday, June 14, 1975
Binghamton, New York

Idea of the escapee (LePan, Lapanne?) being attacked at the end of
the novel, the townspeople assuming it to be a govt attack on the
sky.

Sunday, June 15, 1975
Binghamton, New York

boundary 2 lamb roast at Bob Pawlikowski's big old house in the
country. Site of a 19th century local spa. A stream running under
the house. Under a barn and a house become one building. Bill
Spanos and I bought a whole lamb at Tedeschi's Market. I cut
down three ironwood trees with an inadequate axe and found out
what ironwood is all about. We pushed the spit through the lamb.
Spanos, in the best manner of a Greek mountain rebel, rubbed sage
and thyme on the lamb, all the while drinking Greek wine. We
turned the lamb over a fire, hour after hour. All the while drinking
Greek wine. We played horseshoes and drank wine. We welcomed
guests and drank wine. We fed the guests and drank wine. We
played Pawlikowski's collection of a couple of dozen drums,
African and European, inventing a new version of organized noise,
all the while drinking wine. We saw our guests off into the night, all
the while drinking wine.

Sunburn. Blisters. A hangover, somewhere in the middle of the
afternoon, that could only be cured by more wine. Had a great time.

Tuesday, June 17, 1975
Binghamton, New York

Meg fell out of a tree today and broke an arm. She and another girl, climbing. Boys on the ground, teasing. She is absolutely brave, reasonable. So beautiful I wanted to cry. In the midst of it all she realized a cast meant she couldn't go swimming in the ocean (North Carolina) next week. Began to think of ways to get around the problem — a big plastic bag seemed the best solution. Her friends gathered around her, laughing.

Monday, June 23, 1975
Ottawa, Ontario

My cousin's wife, Francoise, a psychologist, took me to a home for mentally retarded adults. The warmth and dedication evident in the place turned my anxiety into pleasure. A figure in the novel, JG, based on those children kept at home by their parents, on the prairies, in the early stages of homesteading. A face that is only beautiful, a boy who never grows old — because he is free of language.

Sunday, July 13, 1975
Qu'Appelle Valley, Saskatchewan

Lorna Uher met my flight in Regina. We drove to Indian Head, to the experimental station, so I could look at trees. Here on the prairie. The tree that JG climbs when he tries to enter heaven. Stopped in town and I slept for a while on the grass, in the shade of a small tree, in front of the post office. Getting used to being back. The buzz of silence. Sun. To Fort San by late afternoon. The excitement of a group of writers sitting down together at a long table in the dining hall. We made it. Once more. We're here, together. We're here.

Monday, July 14, 1975
Fort Qu'Appelle, Saskatchewan

Rudy Wiebe here as visiting writer this summer. He seems to write a novel a day. Lorna Uher has millions of new poems. Ken Mitchell has 77 plays on the stage. They ask what I've done on my novel. A few more sentences, I explain.

Missed a great nude swim last week, they tell me. People wearing nothing but the green slime from the lake.

To the Lipton beer parlor for a glass of consolation and some country & western on the juke box. A game or two of shuffleboard. Then off to a dance at The Squire, in Fort Qu'Appelle.

Tuesday, July 15, 1975
Qu'Appelle Valley, Saskatchewan

To The Squire again tonight. Because last night was so much fun. More women than men in our group, so we danced in a great mad circle around Anne Szumigalski. The poet of elfin and wicked love Luring us into impossible flight. We circled, raising our arms, clapping to the wild music. Shouting. Sweating. A dance into dancing. I was vaguely horny, pursuing a young actress. I was dancing.

I hurt my back.

An old back injury. One day — one day in the summer of 1950 I would guess — unloading freight in Aklavik. Unloading boxes of boneless beef from a walk-in refrigerator. The two deckhands couldn't find the shipment. I went into the refrigerator, found the shipment, tossed a series of 100-pound boxes out the door to the deckhands. Macho. Hurt my back.

Wednesday, July 16, 1975
Qu'Appelle Valley, Saskatchewan

Softball game this evening. Tall, skinny Reg Silvester wearing his special red softball cap. Rudy Wiebe determined to hit homeruns or nothing. And so I had to do just as well or better. And so I made my sore back worse.

Went to the Lipton Hotel, after the game. Quarters in the juke box and beer on the table. And Tang. For Rudy. He was arguing loudly about the game; we secretly asked the barmaid to threaten to throw him out of the bar. Then we steady and honest drinkers rushed to his defense. We insisted he was suffering from a Tangover.

Thursday, July 17, 1975
Qu'Appelle Valley, Saskatchewan

And in the midst of it, everyone working hard. Writing. This Saskatchewan work ethic. The sound of typewriters, in our dormitory, from dawn to whenever it is I fall asleep. The word-machines, eating paper, talking through the walls.

A long discussion at breakfast this morning. Mealtime a time when we escape those typewriters. Writertalk. This morning: on dating someone whose age is vastly different from your own. Margo, the actress, changing her age before our eyes. Metamorphosis. The other writers, so unable in real life to be anything but themselves. Perhaps with the exception of Ralph Ring, slightly built, endlessly attractive to women, endlessly perambulating. He doesn't walk around from place to place, he perambulates. A poet at once untrained and gifted. While Robert Currie walks. He can only walk, never perambulate. Ralph Ring, finding edges. Robert Currie, working out of an experience of place that was so profound he carries it all, balances the whole thing on his shoulders, as he walks.

Lorna Uher, the poet, almost springs into the air as she walks. I was wrong. She too knows metamorphosis. At each step she runs the risk of becoming a bird.

And Gertrude Story, who was here last year. She travels by appearing and disappearing. She knows how to do it. Disappear. Appear. Disappear.

Friday, July 18, 1975
Qu'Appelle Valley, Saskatchewan

This morning Rudy and I went for a long walk. I teach in the afternoons. The two of us on a prairie hillside overlooking Echo Lake, half expecting Big Bear to ride by. We talked, sitting on a rock in the sun. Then picking our fill of saskatoons. Talk of history — his knowing the history of this valley so well, the stones listened. The wind fell off, into silence. It was like that.

To Regina tonight, with Rudy and his family, with Lorna, to see the Riel play. Rudy and I on the jury. Comic moment when the costume lady, downstairs in a crowd of people, handed me a pair of trousers and told me to change. "Where?" I said. "If you're shy," she said, "go to the bathroom." Rudy: "So this is the studhorse man."

We thought Rudy might try to change the verdict. Not so, he said....His sense of history as something as real as the landscape itself.

Saturday, July 19, 1975
Qu'Appelle Valley, Saskatchewan

Sports Day in Lipton. The Qu'Appelle writers entered a softball team in the competition. We played the somewhat amused, somewhat astonished team from the Standing Buffalo Indian Reserve. The Sioux won.

Then we supported them in their next game. Cheering mightily. But they lost. We were friends in defeat. We lost even more, money this time, at the crown and anchor wheel. We went for a beer.

In fact, some of us drove to Dysart, the next town west of Lipton. Ten miles. On the off-chance that Mary and Wally, in the hotel there, might be serving pyrogies. No pyrogies. But one writer, stepping out of the beer parlor to get some fresh air, carrying an open bottle of beer, encountered a young mountie and the vagaries of prairie law. We lost another twenty-three dollars. Had to organize a raffle of books to raise the money.

Sunday, July 20, 1975
Qu'Appelle Valley, Saskatchewan

No classes on Sunday. A group of us drove north, past Lipton, in search of the old Jewish cemetery. Lipton was originally a settlement established by the Jewish agrarian movement. The straight gravel road bends abruptly. To pass around the cemetery and its dead. The old graves, covered with what look like miniature houses. The names of the dead, crudely printed. Around the graves, the prairie grass neatly mowed. Virgin prairie, with all its flowers. The buckbrush and the wolf willow pressing in at the fence.

Tuesday, July 22, 1975
Qu'Appelle Valley, Saskatchewan

Went up out of the valley to talk with a wonderful beekeeper, Romanchuk, and his wife. Mr. Romanchuk arriving as we arrived; he'd been out picking saskatoons with his small son. Mrs. Romanchuk had just finished extracting. I tasted fresh honey. I was shown a queen. I watched the bees at work....Beekeepers, their total involvement in the mystery. A sense of folktale. A special knowledge of each season and its blossoms. Stories, always, of swarming.

Thursday, July 24, 1975
Qu'Appelle Valley, Saskatchewan

A softball game on the Sioux Reserve. Return match. Again, we lost. We scored two runs because the Indian players were too polite to catch a ball hit by a woman player....After, I talked with three little boys. They wouldn't tell me their names, kept giving each other different names, claiming different names for themselves. They asked what I do. I tried to explain. They looked puzzled. Then one of them said: "Ah. You're like my grandmother. She's a legender."

Tonight, in the dormitory lounge, being lazy, we talk of being legenders. Pat Krause, in her stories, as direct as the color of a shotgun barrel. Steve Scriver, discovering in his poems the language of the hockey arena, all that outcry of language. And Byrna Barclay, our story-mother, retelling her novel, rewriting, retelling.

Friday, July 25, 1975
Qu'Appelle Valley, Saskatchewan

Picnic in a coulee in a cow pasture. Cowshit all around. Bales of straw in a circle around the fire. We told stories, sang. Byrna Barclay, in the falling dark, held us spellbound with an Indian tale. Then it was my turn. But I couldn't tell a story. The novelist unable to tell a story. The ghost of my father, there in the shadows — the story-teller. I sang a song, "Cigareets and Whiskey and Wild Wild Women."

Train went by, filled the whole night with its passing.

David Johnson of Blackearth Percussion, filling the night with two small drums. The cows, too, joining us. Listening.

Sunday, July 27, 1975
Regina, Saskatchewan

Drove to Grenfell, then to Wolseley, with Steve Scriver, to see his father's old print shop. Closed now. The sort of place in which Liebhaber works, in my novel. Beautiful, exciting, scary. The drawers full of type, the many machines. Wordhoard, wordplace. Steve worked here as a boy, helping his father; his father running a newspaper, a community leader, one of the minds behind the rise of the CCF....Supper with Steve and Barb. Then into Regina. To catch a flight back to Binghamton.

Friday, August 22, 1975
Niagara Falls, Ontario

Left Binghamton today. To drive to Calgary, where I'm to be writer-in-residence at the University of Calgary from September through Christmas, then on to the University of Lethbridge....Like trying to leave the earth's gravitational field —

Left Binghamton shortly after 12 noon. Stopped in a roadside rest area west of Owego. I couldn't go on. And I couldn't go back....

Drove to Niagara Falls. Hellish vision — trying to drive into the falls area — wate. ut up by fire — people become cars — garish motels designed by someone who had only seen movies of motels, never slept in one —

Saturday, August 23, 1975
Stratford, Ontario

Fruit stands in a cluster beside the road to Hamilton. Stopped and bought cherries, blackberries. Just walked around, looking at the stands, the people. Fruit in season, ever since I was a child, a kind of reassurance. Cycle. Return. B.C. fruit, coming into Alberta on the train. Boxes stacked on the dray. The phone call from the merchant, they're in. Women canning. Peaches. Apricots. Plums. Pears. The sealers in the copper boiler. The empty crates for me to play with. The women too busy to watch the kids. The beckoning smells in the kitchen, all day long. Then rows of canned fruit, of jam, of jelly, on the wooden shelves in the basement. Canning time.

Managed to get a ticket in Stratford — *Twelfth Night.* Disappointing second half. But fascinating on the clown-fool figure.

Took a room in a house. Canopy over the bed. Old Ontario brick house. Canopied bed. Sleeping fool.

Monday, August 25, 1975
Mildmay, Ontario

Drove to Bamberg, Ontario, today. William Kieswetter, in the little country store, when asked about the Kroetsch family — "John Kroetsch owned the land you are standing on."

The first settling place of the Kroetsch family in the New World. Circa 1830. Exactly 66 1/3 acres, including the farm and the watermill. A widow and her sons, six or seven, migrating from Bavaria.

"The millsite now is a club-site," Kieswetter said. A small man, old, pleased that I had sought out the place, and pained too. "Don't go look."

And after my long search, I didn't.

Wednesday, August 27, 1975
Penetang, Ontario

Visiting with Jim and Elisabeth Bacque, at their summer home on Georgian Bay. A deck in front of the cottage; a long breakfast and talk of books, the three of us lazy in the sun. Jim and I took his powerboat out to North Watcher Island to talk to the fisherman who lives there, Henri Lepage. High waves, to the point of danger. The machismo bond. Then the island, the little kingdom of the fisherman. The Crusoe-world.

Friday, August 29, 1975
North of Lake Superior, Ontario

Stopped in Iron Bridge last night; a combination of truck traffic and wind-driven rain made driving suicidal. Up this morning at five. Read page proofs of *Badlands* for an hour. Drove 720 miles today.

Sunday, August 31, 1975
Calgary, Alberta

Stopped last night with Steve Scriver, his wife Barb and their two children, in Grenfell, Saskatchewan. Went to the beer parlor. A town blest with stories. And with a poet who will interpret them onto the page.

Woke up at 6 a.m. and tiptoed out of the lovely old Scriver house. Drove to Calgary. Stan and Philomena Hauck have found an apartment for me. A delightful, large, quiet place. I'm exhausted.

Saturday, September 6, 1975
Vermilion, Alberta

Talked with Harley Youngberg about ice-cutting. He spent many winters in Edmonton and then out in Jasper National Park, with an ice-cutting gang. In the novel, a figure who makes his living harvesting ice.

Sunday, September 7, 1975
Vermilion, Alberta

Drove up to Frog Lake. A few dozen garter snakes, sunning themselves on the road. Hard to avoid driving over them.

Three Indians at the memorial marker, one of them using a "treasure finder" on the grounds around the marker.

Thursday, September 11, 1975
Calgary, Alberta

Dinner tonight with John and Kay Snow and friends. In a perfect old Calgary house, downtown, a house full of art. Crammed full of travel and creation. John a printmaker, painter, sculptor. A vision of landscape in vast and subtle dialectic with hesitant, unstoppable people. That pressure in the Canadian to do it, and to see at the same time some sort of futility at the doing. Never somehow achieving the conviction that achievement is worth it. The *ha* at one's own working. The way John shows us the prodigious consequence, the red and yellow and blue consequence of his bending over cold stone. That tall, tall man, bent over those blank blocks of stone. To touch. Lovingly.

Friday, September 12, 1975
Calgary, Alberta

Went to the zoo. To look at seals. I'm working on a poem, something that struck me when I was driving through the Maritimes, researching the background of Hazard Lepage.

Saturday, September 13, 1975
Strawberry Creek, Alberta

Lorna Uher flew to Calgary from Regina, then we drove north to Rudy Wiebe's farm, on Strawberry Creek, west of Leduc some 30-odd miles. His camp in a fine stand of trees, on a high bank above the creek. The tribes gathering.

A CBC television crew arrives, to film Rudy and me talking beside the creek. In the natural sun. For a program on Canadian culture. Jesse Nishihata in charge. He climbs out of the van, offers us four cases of beer. Four dozen bottles. Rudy explains that he allows no beer or liquor on his land. Smiles of disbelief. Look, Rudy says, I don't allow NObody to bring alcoholic refreshments on my land. Right, I say to the astonished driver, I'll show you where to cache the stuff, outside the gate, until you leave. And I follow alongside the van. And I whisper, Will you sell us a couple of cases? This has got to be the driest quarter-section west of Thunder Bay. You can have a couple, the driver says, I see you're suffering. So I hide two cases in a brushpile. Shannon Twofeathers arrives. Maria Campbell arrives. No one can persuade Rudy to relent. The beer is getting warm, maybe even spoiling.

Sitting around the fire that night, our throats parched, we try to sing. Then Rudy spills a kettle of hot water, scalding Lorna's feet. We drive her to a doctor. We come back and crawl into our sleeping bags, nine of us in a homemade A-frame. Lorna is in pain. I admit to having a bottle of rye in my car, brought with me purely for medicinal purposes. Rudy relents. In the darkness, we pass the medicine to whomsoever might need a swallow.

Tuesday, October 14, 1975
Calgary, Alberta

Met with Hal Dahlie and his graduate class — discussed Lowry's "Through the Panama." That overwhelming story. Lowry caught between his conviction that it's impossible to write a novel and his need to write the last, all-saying novel. The language itself deconstructed out of the story — and back in. And Hal himself somehow a part of the story's meaning. Born in Norway, taken to Holden, Alberta, as a child, by his homesteading parents. The family driven by the 30s to Smithers, B.C., to a log house in the forest. Hal, at 16, working on a lighthouse tender, then for three months living on the southernmost island of the Queen Charlotte's as a lighthouse keeper. The Lowry connection.

Thursday, November 6, 1975
Winnipeg, Manitoba

Gave a reading at noon today at the University of Manitoba. Ron Smith and John Marshall here, from Oolichan Books, Lantzille, B.C., distributing my new book, *The Stone Hammer Poems*. A maelstrom of energy, this place. Especially St. John's College. A tall tale, roaring place. David Arnason and Dennis Cooley and Robert Enright like some strange triumvirate of voicemen, booting silence out of heaven. Ken Hughes as a presiding spirit made flesh and thirsty. Radio interviews in progress. Books being published. And to top it off, a party in Arnason's house with Al Purdy and W. O. Mitchell in a wonderful lying contest, with each insisting that he is the master of truth.

Saturday, November 15, 1975
Heisler, Alberta

Fiftieth wedding anniversary of Philip and Gertrude Hauck, in Heisler. My hometown. Like being inside my novel — the extended family, drawn together. A day and night of food, talk, dance, celebration. The talk of generations. The giving of gifts. The making of speeches. Philip's family, like my father's, from Ontario. Gertrude's family, like my mother's, from the States. From across the line, as they say. The migration of families, of groups of families. The continuity.

Bob Moorehead telling how once he drove a herd of cattle over me, when I was a small child, playing out of sight behind a corner of our machine shed. Aunt Mary O'Connor and others telling me I was the most spoiled child in the community, because of my doting parents. Philip and Gertie, parents to us all, now.

Wednesday, November 26, 1975
Calgary, Alberta

A dinner honoring Brian Moore; the Library, University of Calgary, officially receiving his papers. He's a witty, attractive man at the dinner table, at once gentle and acerbic. We talked of writing about a place while living somewhere else, as he has done for years; his conviction that living away keeps the vision whole, the place complete. But I begin to wonder....I sat between his wife Jean and Betty Dahlie and didn't want the dinner to end.

Wednesday, December 3, 1975
Calgary, Alberta

Drove to Banff to have coffee with Jon Whyte. Slippery roads, because of a chinook. Jon writing new, daring poems, up there on his mountain perch. A mountain man, with mountain ancestors. Mountains, almost, as ancestors. His sense of history issuing into the surreal, the found poem, the concrete poem. The narrative poem.

Driving back through the territory where Altman has been making a movie. An old man who is working with me, writing poems, was employed on the Altman set all summer. Altman took one look at him, a retired farmer who now works as a guide in the mountains most summers — Altman took one look, listened, gave him some notes and told him to go sit by the river and write his own script. Must try that with a character in a novel.

Thursday, December 25, 1975
Petaluma, California

Christmas with Sheila, here, just north of San Francisco. A huge old-fashioned Christmas dinner. Like home on the prairies. But Sheila had to mow her grass yesterday. Getting ready for Santa Claus.

Thursday, January 8, 1976
Lethbridge, Alberta

Getting used to being here. As writer-in-residence at the university. Liking the small-city feel (45,000), the landscape (snow, sun, space, and the beautiful, stark valley of the Oldman River — the Blackfoot trickster Old Man, his river). Liking the university itself, the great long Erickson building, splendid and ship-layered in the coulees. Liking the old house I live in, a four-bedroom house, crammed with antiques and plants. A house with lovely wooden floors. And floors somehow make a house. Two studies; instead I work at the round oak table in the dining room. Laurie Ricou, the departmental chairman, a delightful person, inclined to work too hard. But he plays hard too. He'll introduce me to the students by having me give a short reading, followed by a question period, followed by two kegs of beer.

The secretary put a notice on my door: I'm not to be bothered any morning, ever: she will take all messages, arrange appointments. A wonderful woman who worked for years as a secretary for the United Church — she cannot understand why Ricou swears so much. And the day I arrived I materialized out of my office, went to her, asked if it was Monday or Tuesday. She still hasn't come to terms with that one.

Friday, March 12, 1976
Lethbridge, Alberta

My need to be the outsider. Rushed back here from two Ontario readings, in order to recover my secrecy. Last night on the flight from Toronto to Calgary — I thought again of a poem, "The Bullshit/Artist." On riding the poetry circuit. The clown/fool/preacher. At 39,000 feet, all those sleeping bodies, the dim light, the roar of the plane and the silence too. The poet himself, hurtled home. Hurtling. The moved and unmoving mover.

Stayed in a motel in Calgary. Caught a Time Airways flight this morning. To hear Miriam Waddington read at noon. Her nagging, eloquent poems, why don't you love me, you prick?

Curious, how we allow so much sexuality in novels, in plays, yet there is so little in poetry. In a form that is supposedly lyric. About an experience that is supposedly lyric.

44

Sunday, April 4, 1976
Lethbridge, Alberta

For the moment I'm solving my problems by working too hard....Last night, went to campus, to a Blackfoot Pow-wow. The trance induced by the drumming, by the wailed and chanted songs. I wanted to get up and dance with the dancers, their faces stonily indifferent, their bodies in motion. The past, in all its distortions, so present here.

Going to a hockey game tonight, with Ricou and Latta. Bill Latta a kind of controlled D. H. Lawrence figure. A big man, writing precise, exquisitely cared-for poems.

Novel: Father Basil, the day he arrived in Big Indian, decided these people should be given extreme unction at the time of birth, baptism at the time of death, and for the next forty years...

the phantom buffalo
the snow-covered bull

bull's blood — used for divination

Friday, April 9, 1976
Lethbridge, Alberta

Back last night from Castlegar, B.C. Flew in there from Calgary. The plane goes down a river valley, with mountains on both sides, makes a sharp left turn around a hump, a shoulder of mountain, a cliff. We turned. A small plane crossed the landing field when we were almost down. Great surge of engine power. Great surge of adrenaline. Got down next try, and I lectured myself on loving the earth, not the sky. Came time to drive to Fred Wah's mountainside house — a mud slide had closed the road. Had to drive 65 miles to go 15. On mountain roads. Next day I lectured myself on loving the sky.

Fred Wah a kind of ideal poet, his integrity of vision, his not looking away from the light of the word itself. Not the mere Word, but the word itself. Pauline Wah the embodiment of clarity. She thinks with her whole being. Her body's being thinks poems. The Kootenay.

Read most of *Invisible Cities* (Calvino) on various planes.

We are a people who have not dreamed.
Imagine that.

Rhys Carpenter, *Folk Tales, Fiction and Saga in the Homeric Epics*, p.125: "Sisyphos boasted that he could escape death..."

Liebhaber: Perhaps death too will grow old and die.

He took to stepping into any cowpie he saw, and people began to wonder.

Robert Kroetsch in Lethbridge, 1976   *photo by Julia Berry*

47

The lamb roast at Bob Pawlikowski's big, old house in the country on June 15, 1975. Left to right: Bob Pawlikowski, Bill Spanos and Robert Kroetsch.

Students and staff at the Saskatchewan School of the Arts in 1974. Left to right: Robert Kroetsch, Gertrude Story, Ken Mitchell, Sharon Maier, Harry Mitchell, Byrna Barclay, Mary Ann Seitz, Margaret Herrington, Reg Silvester.

Photo by Graphic Photo Studio
Fort Qu'Appelle, Sask.

Lorna Uher   photo by Julia Berry

Tuesday, April 13, 1976
Lethbridge, Alberta

Old Coyote. Andy Suknaski calls me Old Coyote, I'm told by George Melnyk. Old Coyote is writing a lot of poems. Old Coyote keeps a few dens, I'm told, ain't going to get himself caught.

This year, so far: 46 airplane flights.

Not the writing of my novel; the inching of my novel.

Jerry Lapanne never gets to Rita. He dies, finally, for love: possibly for murder. Charged with murder and rape. He insists to the end it was his brother (identical twin) who raped the girl; he killed his brother trying to save her.

The obscenity of art is not in the specifics that offend a school trustee in Southern Ontario; rather, it's in the sight of the artist himself, the novelist, observing the stains in his hero's shorts, watching his hero shave, checking to see if his heroine has menstruated this month. Perhaps we think of poetry as superior to fiction simply because the poet doesn't have to think of these matters.

51

Wednesday, April 14, 1976
Lethbridge, Alberta

I cannot at the moment believe that writing is worth it to the writer.

Why is the sternum
in front?
Are we, perchance,
proceeding backwards?

Snow moving in, from the north. I'm to drive to the badlands.
Michael Ondaatje arriving tomorrow. Maybe the old chasm will
help, the eye leaping into the badlands canyon. Deadlodge, it's
called.

From my office window, a snow fence. Like a seam that holds
together earth and sky.

I look at my hands.
They are no longer my own.
They have become my father's
hands.

What happened last night?

Terry & Caroline Heath and their three sons stayed with me last night. This morning, a fine discussion of Canadian writing. Terry insisting we have no tradition and must write out of that. My asserting against his statement a belief in the text beneath the text, an everlasting grope into the shape of that darkness. As with rural people, the complexities and patterns beneath the formulaic speech. Almost the opposite of urban, where the surface is sometimes more complicated than what lies beneath it. But the text beneath the text, as in *Gone Indian*, is at the root of our Canadian writing. The ur-novel that no ONE will ever write.

I. Reed, in *The Black Aesthetic*: "But there were always the prophet-necromancers whose folk tales and sermons defied the conventions of plot, conflict, causality, and motivation..."

Yesterday, driving to Medicine Hat to meet a class — somewhere between Purple Springs and Seven Persons, the sky open and shut, I stopped and wrote of L:

In the soft windmill
of your body
I dream

Monday, April 26, 1976
Lethbridge, Alberta

Talking with Terry Heath last week: his remarking that the visit is the central western Canadian art (language) form.

I've been working on a poem, *Seed Catalogue*, instead of on the novel.

I was tired of work and drove out to a small town, Picture Butte, and sat in the chinaman's, watching the wind blow, watching the smalltown people come in to drink coffee, listening to their humor, their yarns.

Michael Ondaatje, visiting. Our walking in the badlands. His taking photos. His mind there, pristinely at work, making a film script of my novel, *Badlands*. The absolute of his attention.

Lorna Uher, visiting. Your poem is your woman, she tells me.

The only way I can write poems
is by not being a poet.

Tuesday, May 4, 1976
Lethbridge, Alberta

Plotting the end of the novel. The woman who loved bees: perhaps, it turns out, she *is* immortal.

The great union that perpetuates the world. The experience that Web (almost) had, in the tornado, in *Badlands*.

Attempt to unite sensuality and immortality.

Heroes are the real clowns of our world.

Liebhaber's endless "good" ideas, suggestions, plans — beginning with his attempt to take Martin Lang home. All of them powered by his wish to defeat death.

I guess I did put something down on paper, after all, in spite of all my flying around. And as it turns out, flying is central to the book; the idea of flying. Of falling....As usual. In spite of my ferocious inventing of worlds....I feel pretty good. And yet I hate this writing of a first draft more than anything else. Now I can begin what Joyce called the "layering"; the exploration of implication, the play with design.

Yeats. I'm reading Yeats again. Yeats, along with a bit of Dickens. Don't ask me what the connection might be....I like the energy on each page of Dickens, the...Where was I? Oh yes, nowhere...The novel exists. It is quite literally here, on my desk. Now, in another year, I can write it....

Thursday, May 6, 1976
Lethbridge, Alberta

Paul Thompson of Theatre Passe Muraille here today. He's interested in making a play of *The Studhorse Man*, complete with stage-horses. A stallion. And he's doing research on a play he's producing in Quebec. We drove out to see traces of the old trail south. Wagon tracks down into a coulee, tracks worn deep in the prairie. We went to Fort Whoop-Up. Thompson, hour after hour, leaping from idea to idea. Into the museum. Then we found ourselves drinking with a group of Hutterites, in a beer parlor. They were in town, allowed away from the colony once every two weeks. The young men, talking about sex: the sexual delight of plucking geese with young women. Thompson and I realizing that once again there was something good and basic that we'd missed out on.

Thursday, May 20, 1976
Lethbridge, Alberta

Houses. I'm into the house-appreciating side of myself. Living in Laurie and Treva Ricou's house now. This new, bare place, after the Read/antique house. After the luxury of accumulation, the luxury of simplicity. The Ricous have moved out most of their furniture, making room for renters who are to arrive in July. I have no furniture that I can't carry in my car. I like the clarity. I like, here, the arrangement of rooms, the order of corners, the page-like veracity of walls....

I miss the Ricous. Treva's extravagant meals, destroying my satisfaction with bachelorhood; her sharp wit, aimed at the folly of all our studying. Ricou taking his family to Ottawa for a year, where he'll do research. On notions of childhood in literature. That place in time.

Genius loci. Is not landscape an event as well as a setting? The place of mythology, of story, become action.

June, 1976
Lethbridge, Alberta

George Melnyk and his wife drove down from Edmonton to interview me for *Q & Q*. Camping along the way. Driving in their old VW. Camera and writing pad, the romance of road journalism. But for all that, George fascinated by houses. He reads my various houses, decodes them, tells me where I'm at and where I'm headed (home). And I decode his decoding, see that while he tents out he too is headed towards a mortgage.

George, with his gentleness, his concern for right action (left), his need to be unacademic, his efforts to remain vaguely Ukrainian, his temptation to enter into history — again and again, it is he who bumbles into flight, gives the rest of us his clumsy dance of direction. His wise wife, Julia Berry, taking pictures.

Friday, July 9, 1976
Qu'Appelle Valley, Saskatchewan

The pleasure of return.

Jim Ellemers in charge, distanced from the world by his pipe. A man who learned, somehow, from the art of painting, a way to space all these people together. While the rest of us locate ourselves by a restless mapping, the quick, one-before-supper trip to Lebret. That bar, overlooking the lake, under the hill where The Stations of the Cross climb to the sky.

O Word of Eliot
  we cannot believe you
O Principle of Causality
  we cannot believe you
O Verisimilitude
  we cannot believe you
O Depth & Profundity
  we cannot believe you
O Epiphany of Joyce
  we cannot believe you

That Indian, in the bar, potbellied and laughing, challenging Steve Scriver to a game of shuffleboard, beating the pants off him while I watched and got an idea and Steve squirmed and then laughed and we all tried a mixture of Tang and dark rum.

The horses are singing.

Saturday, July 10, 1976
Qu'Appelle Valley, Saskatchewan

Hugh Hood here to teach prose writing. He knows by heart all the statistics about baseball and quotes them without provocation. He comes equipped with seven pairs of expensive sneakers, colors various, many sweat suits and baseball caps and a couple of gloves. We went out to play ball. He can't catch or throw or hit. The novelist as amateur. He'll probably write a great sports novel.

Ed Dyck, who is what happens to literature after postmodern. The leap from logic into linguistics into poetry. And Brenda Riches: a woman who works quite the other way, from 19th century sentimentalism towards a sense of the glimpsed, the fragmentary, the floating phrase that is at once as new as glass, as perpetual as an empty popcorn bowl.

The friendship I feel with Byrna Barclay, our shared admiration for Rudy Wiebe and his passionate belief that he can know, her own dedication to the pulse of language. Lorna Uher: mothering herself savagely into poethood. Steve Scriver: the athlete as poet, winning a phrase out of chaos.

The nighttime drive to the Dysart Hotel. Stars and darkness, and the road like a dream; out of the dark then, into the sudden light of the beer parlor. That Canadian name for getting warm on a chilly day, for flirting, for making out, for hiding, for meeting, for sitting down, for telling a story.

Tuesday, September 7, 1976
Winnipeg, Manitoba

Just got here one hour ago.

I hate arrivals
as much as I hate
departures.

What do I do next?

Wednesday, September 22, 1976
Winnipeg, Manitoba

The function of chaos: what is it?

The nuisance grounds.

Still in my Pembina Highway motel. Waiting to get into a big house
in Wildwood, on the Red River. The owners preparing to go to
Florida for the winter. I'm up early each morning. Listen to traffic
and to CBC radio while I shower, dress, make coffee, read a book at
the small table in my small kitchen. Reading Dorn. Spicer.
Calvino.   Ondaatje....CBC the boon of morning....To be a
Canadian: a fate so barren and so complicated I can hardly endure.

Seed Catalogue will become a book. Thanks to Turnstone Press
and those four adventurers: Arnason, Cooley, Enright, John
Beaver. They dare to be culture-makers, the givers of new form, in a
city that prides itself on having grown old young. When *high*
culture threatens to become fossilized — when it threatens to
become mere imitation of distant culture, the prophets come into
town. From Gimli. From Estevan. From Saskatoon. And John
Beaver, a scholar from Britain who studies French-Canadian
writing. Making it new.

Sunday, September 26, 1976
Winnipeg, Manitoba

Went to a party. I bombed out, failed in every way. A guest, after ten minutes of monologuing at me, asked point blank if I had anything to say. I fled to the side of a pretty girl. Her third sentence was, Do you sky-dive? For a wild moment I thought there was something new in sex that I was about to discover. But no: the pretty girl was on her way to North Dakota to spend a day jumping out of airplanes. I was horny, for a moment I wavered, thinking maybe I could, maybe I could just step out of an airplane, figure it out on the way down, hoping to impress the woman, get laid. We discussed, briefly, techniques used in packing a parachute. Another man joins us, obviously on the make, he begins to tell about how once he just packed his parachute in a Safeway shopping bag, unpacked it as he was falling. I left the party early.

Today, again, for the third time: to the art gallery and the Hermitage paintings: my security blanket. Fetti's "Portrait of an Actor" (17th cent): the old entertainer, the light almost too bright on his forehead; and in the darkness beneath, his hand holding an almost-unnoticed black mask. Time & art: you/better believe it. Or the horse in Poussin's "Tancred and Erminia"; the terrible white horse. Or Velazquez' "The Repast." Simply, eating. And yet that meal so complicated, so much our everything.

Wednesday, September 29, 1976
Winnipeg, Manitoba

Somewhere, in the darkness, I went to Wertmuller's film, *Seven Beauties*: a stunning (yes)...the actuality of the psyche. ? . Then, last night, I went to the unveiling (if that's the word) of a new painting by a young Cree Indian artist, Jackson Beardy. He and I were both gloriously bored and got into a corner and started talking. I came away humbled by what it means to be an artist. He had, as a young man, first to get permission from his tribal elders to paint the sacred symbols. Then, having proved that he deserved permission, he had to be led to understand: a journey with the medicine men, like a candidate learning to be a shaman. And now, each time he paints a picture: the burden of tribal speech.

Friday, October 8, 1976
Winnipeg, Manitoba

First reading of "Seed Catalogue." It works as a poem. All that bloody gambling. It WORKS! We drank for ten hours, in the campus pub, after the reading — four of us at the hard core, but many others floating in and out. A rare and beautiful drunk....I was in love for 20 minutes, then the woman vanished, simply vanished....Robert Enright a kind of lost Renaissance prince, presiding at the table, his infinite women coming to bless us with their beauty....Dennis Cooley, his puns beginning to pun on the puns....Arnason, splendid and alone and tortured in his father-role to the world....George Morrisette, making us laugh at his agony....The ghost of Suknaski at the table, the recurring talk of his talking poems, his story poems, his counterpoint to our raging, that far Wood Mountain.

writing a novel is brutal physical work. Brutal brutal. I'm sick of it. I quit. Right now, this minute, at thirty-one minutes past eleven in the morning, Tuesday, October twelve, 1976, I just goddamned QUIT (QUIT) I can't stand it my back aches my head aches from holding my eyes I QUIT no human being should be allowed to do such a thing as write a novel   i can't go on i'm on the third   the thirteenth   version of chapter 3   years, it will take me years to complete this monstrosity the characters keep changing maybe they're just growing old it's taking me so long to write the book damnit yes they grow old on me while I slave

i can't get used to this damned expensive electric typewriter but the trouble is i can't bring myself to stop using it because i'm able to go so fast on it but

even, going fast, it will take me ten years to write this novel i hate every damned anchored and printed word every syllable every letter and blotch that finds its way onto the decency of the white page

i can't go on

my ears ache from listening to the typewriter making words my whole being   what being?   yes, isn't it nice to suppose we have a being   a novelist is a lumberjack a dock worker and a coal miner rolled into one a

i can't
i
cant
go
o
n
.

Saturday, October 23, 1976
Winnipeg, Manitoba

Phil Butterfield, the philosopher, the true genuine philosopher, showed up unexpectedly from the University of Lethbridge, that utter genius at enjoying the occasion, this very minute of this very living. Phil Butterfield showed up out of nowhere, bursting with stories, Christ it was good to hear the man. His trip to Europe, Phil, hurtling down an English road, driving on the "wrong" side — "I gave up all my dignity. I begged my wife to let me go home" — Phil ranting on while half the patrons in the expensive restaurant eavesdropped, Phil, talking about English cathedrals, his desperate lostness, the beautiful heifer he's going to show in Regina, the attractions of Norwegian life, the night we burned the old barn on his ranch, there on the Oldman River, Bill Latta's pneumonia (he's recovering), the dullness of Copenhagen, a stripper he's heard about in Winnipeg, the fact that he knows more about Aristotle's *Poetics* than any scholar alive, a friend of his who could hear footprints.

The eagle in my novel. I stole that from Butterfield's ranch. We were out walking one day, loking at tipi rings in the prairie grass. The eagle waited, watched us from a hillside, waited.

Monday, December 6, 1976
Winnipeg, Manitoba

yup, got a little pie-eyed at my own party, forgot to serve the cold
cuts to all the Turnstone Press people, the Moose Jaw Movement
poets, and now I have something like 6 pounds of sliced meat to
survive on through the winter   2 pounds of moose baloney that
someone brought along, frozen   i forgot to introduce the guests to
each other   i forgot to remove two candles from the wall, knowing
someone would be tempted to light them, someone did   and now i
have to figure out how to get melted candlewax out of a carpet   but
it was a good party   30 people?   George Amabile saving the day
(night) by playing his guitar and singing   Gary Geddes staying here
for a few days, doing research on the Canadian troops caught in
Hong Kong by the Japanese   Gary the perfect guest, he kept the
show together   carried out a drunk   kept ice in the ice bucket   i
mean, i was useless, the happiest drunk in the world   today, this
morning, six pages of rewrite in two hours   the old guilt trip

Friday, December 17, 1976
Winnipeg, Manitoba

This afternoon I wrote to John Teunissen, Head of the Department of English, University of Manitoba, saying I'd be a candidate for a job. After all my hesitating, the prairies begin, again, to feel like the inevitable home. The journey here...John himself a fine critic and editor, an overwhelming teacher, working on a long, radical study of Hemingway...Evelyn Hinz, editor and critic (of Anais Nin, among others), one of the best teachers I've met anywhere...archetypal critics, a departure, rereading Jung, resisting Frye... David Williams as second-generation, publishing a book, *Faulkner's Women: The Myth and the Muse*...and the energy of the St. John's people, publishing books, magazines...my rented house by the river. All these rented houses. Until I'm tempted to return. A vast rootedness, in spite of everything. The infernal war between the alone and love. A suffering toward.

Monday, February 7, 1977
Winnipeg, Manitoba

The novel, today, has some semblance of novelness. Not so much as to be destroyed by it. Perhaps it flows from the lyric-convention of the opening through the possibilities of rigorous convention into something open, something coming apart, then something almost a lyric poem. As I try to rewrite the ending.

This northern drought. The sadness of a winter landscape with insufficient snow. I want blizzards, of various sorts.

Friday, February 25, 1977
Winnipeg, Manitoba

There is some unexplored territory that I lurch towards, almost unwillingly:

the continuing poem?

the destruction of shape in the novel?

as I strip down the story in the present work —

as I begin to refuse to call it a novel, calling it now only a story: goddamn

I deconstruct even after I've come to the end of deconstruction:

I read successful novels and recoil from even the best of them, from the "rain of detail" that makes books fat

back towards Gass and the heart of the heart of.

Saturday, April 2, 1977
Winnipeg, Manitoba

Today: stuck on the scene where Liebhaber turns over the hull of his boat, and gets trapped beneath it. Then, while making love, late in the afternoon, I heard the crows picking at the overturned hull. Liebhaber began to talk — from his immortality, from his grave — to what he hopes is the talking crow.

Mrs. Aylesworth. The fierce-eyed, redheaded teacher at Red Deer High School who told me I should become a writer. Again, today, I thought of her. My debt to a teacher.

The patriarchal stance. *I* don't have to decide. And so I win my combination of freedom and catastrophe.

Wednesday, April 20, 1977
Winnipeg, Manitoba

I am sick of the tyranny of narrative. And fascinated by the narrative that I'm creating. And that's the whole story.

Monday, April 25, 1977
Winnipeg, Manitoba

Back from the annual festival, Mosaic Massey, in Brandon. On the mass media this year.

So there I was, trying to explain how TV puts you into a state of bodily passivity, into surrender, while radio allows you to (?) — and Marshall breaks in on me; Marshall McLuhans me/ha — his rap about the telephone and no body and all that

and I listened; yes, in the global village, somebody's got to do the listening:

he's a Vegas dealer from waaaaaay back. A riverboat man, even in his dress. A gambler.

Earle Birney was there. He and I sought refuge in remembered lines of poetry. At 73 he's living with a woman of 25, writing fine poems about loving and dying. A man of passion.

Tuesday, May 10, 1977
Winnipeg, Manitoba

Sick. Just plain sick. Caught one hell of a cold at a party at Pierre Berton's house, north of Toronto. After a meeting of the Writers' Union. All day Sunday the wind blew, flakes of snow streaked past the windows without ever getting to the ground, 200 writers and other guests waited to enter the swimming pool and waiting drank punch. A fairly bombed time of it. Heaps of food. Margaret Atwood's baby the star. Berton a huge man, generous, important to the success of the Union, able to conduct four intelligent conversations at once. The house itself a wandering affair that adapts to the edge of the river valley, to the view, to a big man's need for enclosed space.

Need some Hank Williams to cheer me up.

Must read a section of a dissertation on William Carlos Williams. Just finished a dissertation on the meta-naturalism of a number of American novels. SUNY-Bing.

Wednesday, May 11, 1977
Winnipeg, Manitoba

I have come to the chapter where the boy who was reared by coyotes returns to the farm, and I find him speaking pig Latin (apparently) and rather decently dressed. And so: origins. The myth of the founding of the city. De/construction. Destruct/shun.

The meaning that doesn't quite mean. Somewhere, in a chapter that a typist has on her desk, a group of card players recognize, for a moment, that all the numbers and pictures on the cards mean nothing.

I begin to understand that when I begin a novel I am the creator, I control, select, invent. At some point the created world assumes control of the creator. It uses the writer to get itself created, completed. Thus, currently, my loss of identity. I am the merest vehicle, the tool, of my novel's ambition.

I go on reading about bees. The newest temptation: to become, against all this, a beekeeper....But then the bees, so quickly, would make me one of their workers, a part of their design and intent.

The only way to escape: begin to imagine another novel.

I am lost, but that is all. I am only lost. From that, there is a possible finding.

I am blank tonight. The boy raised by the coyotes is more real than I.

Friday, June 17, 1977
Winnipeg, Manitoba

This evening: packing books. Again, I must move. I go to Fort San on July 9. Tonight: coffee, capuccino, at Basil's. Handsome people, talking. I listen.

Heavy rain all day. Thoughts of how it rains in Binghamton. That heavy, everlasting, green Binghamton rain. Warm rain. Not a cooling rain. A sweaty rain.

Current title: *The War Against the Sky*. This morning I rewrote the opening of chapter 3: the introduction of Liebhaber into the story.

Friday, July 15, 1977
Qu'Appelle Valley, Saskatchewan

Homeagain homeagain. This valley, this arts center. A still point. And always changing. Eli Mandel here this summer to teach the writing of poetry. Eli, too, a center. All his caring humanity visible and alive each day. The vision at once comic and tragic. His life itself becoming a model for others: his daring to depart. His daring to return. And his students, with him, writing the "Rules For Poetry" that include:

1. There are no rules.
2. There are rules.

5. Do not throw hot water on a cold pig or cold water on a hot pig (source: M. Ondaatje).

10. A line should be as long as it should be.

Students here or just visiting from past years, this flow of community: Lois Simmie, wringing stories out of remembered solitudes. Gertrude Story, in some opposite way, hearing the edge and clang of the colloquial, letting all her talent speak through the traditions of talk. Geoff Ursell, writing songs, writing experimental stories; both, and equally, testing the shape of artifice. Barbara Sapergia, recovering into her novel a Romanian life that was lived, spent, in terrible silence. Dave Carpenter, playing his banjo at night, refusing all separation of life and art, insisting that he can live both, creating out of lived art an art form that hardly needs the page: which, then, who then, is to be his novel?

Ed Dyck here, for a visit. A math professor turned poet. Poetry turned to language. A refusal of the presence of his life in the poem. Almost. Then, the poem itself reversing itself, consuming him.

Monday, July 18 1977
Qu'Appelle Valley, Saskatchewan

Our theme song, on the juke box in the Lipton Hotel: Wasted Days & Wasted Nights.

Visitors and the absent and the present, all of us around a beer-covered table. Sorestad, giving us his pub poems. Anne Szumigalski, inciting us to dance and to poetry; arrest that woman for disturbing the sleep of the nation. Ken Mitchell, forever in a hurry, appearing almost in a blur, dashing across the continent. Byrna, opening a bag of Cheezies, deep now into the habit of writing. Rooted. We are, in this crossing of our myriad lines, rooted.

So slowly,
we learn to be
lovers.

And the poem of our naming each other. Is Lala back from Victoria? Will Gary visit? I hear that Mary Ann's book is going to be published — *Shelterbelt*; that's the title she settled on. Did Campbell ever finish that poem? Scriver, why did you leave the dirty poems out of *Between the Lines*?...Standing Buffalo....Carry-the-Kettle....Grenfell....Liz Allen, telling us how the crops are this year, giving us the poems of her New Zealand past, of her Saskatchewan farm....Suknaski, forever sulking in the Rockies, insisting that we let him feel neglected, while every day we discuss his vision of ourselves....My four summers, in the place of this place, the exchange of

gifts.

Monday, July 25, 1977
Lantzville, Vancouver Island

Begin: on the ferry
begin

Horseshoe Bay to Nanaimo. *Queen of Nanaimo.* Departed
Horseshoe Bay 1945 hours, Monday, July 25. Nanaimo. The Hub
City of Vancouver Island. The City With the Most Moderate
Climate in North America. The Bathtub Racing Capital of the
World.

The sailing away: an act
of separation. Goodbye,
novel.

Tuesday, July 26, 1977
Lantzville, Vancouver Island

Woke up at nine. In the Smiths' big house on a cliff overlooking Georgia Strait. Ron and Pat and their small daughter Nicole are in England. I'm here for a vacation. Overlooking blue water. Far mountains. Snow on those mainland mountains, across the strait.

To town to buy groceries: potatoes, bacon, eggs, milk, cheddar, brie, Swedish Stilton, lettuce, tomatoes, frozen orange juice, chicken, hamburger, margarine, radishes, canned soup, bread.

Making breakfast at ten-thirty. John Marshall came by. He runs Oolichan Books from the basement of the house, while Ron is away this year, teaching in England.

Went to the liquor store after my late breakfast. A dozen beer. Two bottles of wine. A bottle of vodka.

Prairie people in the beer parlor in the Lantzville Hotel, talking about Lethbridge, Regina, Edmonton. Six people — two couples, a lone man, a lone woman — seated far a part and talking to each other across the empty tables. Planning a visit home. Debating the terrible train trip versus the terrible bus trip. The lone woman saying she can't leave her husband, can't walk out on him, bastard that he is, because she's 62 and has no more choices. The barmaid disagreeing. Then, to me, softly: "Get a row started in here. We'll be in court by this afternoon." The man from Regina tries to ease the tension: he swears to heaven he won't bootleg ever again. His wife's pleasure at his humor.

Thursday, July 28, 1977
Lantzville, Vancouver Island

The sea-sound of the sea. Wind on water on beach. But here around the house, here on the cliff among the huge trees, always, a stillness. The leaves never move on the trees. The effect:

Yes, that's a difference from the prairies. On the prairies the leaves move, even when there seems to be no wind at all, the trees and bushes and grass are alive. The fields of grain shift. The ditches stir.

The spiders thrive in this stillness, the beautiful spiders, over and over, they trap me. They smack their cobwebs onto my glasses. So far, each time, I've escaped, but I know, I know...

Bought a copy of Doris Shadbolt's book/catalogue on Emily Carr. Found, in Ron's library, a copy of Lowry's *Dark as the Grave*...Those two artists, framing our experience. Lowry, from far away, finding. Carr, from this place, exploring.

Friday, July 29, 1977
Long Beach, Vancouver Island

Drove across the island to Long Beach. Stayed in the Wickaninnish Inn. This is to be the last year of operation of the Inn. Pacific Rim National Park. A wilderness area. The berry bushes bigger that people, the ferns as tall as standing bears. Rain forest. The Pacific Ocean, shaping this ecstasy of beach. The standing forest a jungle, the driftwood on the beach a forest. What storm could have lifted the beached logs into these postures?...John Marshall, shaping his long poem, *The West Coast Trail*, out of a path that is hardly there, after a week of nature's growing. The poem of walking.

Saturday, July 30, 1977
Lantzville, Vancouver Island

Departed after a buffet lunch. Feasting on salmon. Drove into Ucluelet to Ukee Days. Talked for a long time with a fisherman, on a boat in a long line of boats. He spoke of a section of the ocean as The Prairies. He told of another fisherman who was out on The Prairies one night in his boat and went to sleep. In the morning when he woke up — his deckhand was gone. Turned around and went back for miles, for hours. But never found him....I understand that about the prairies, how you could lose a man out there.

Watched the log-rolling competition. Ate fish and chips. Walked around in the short stories of Jack Hodgins. Left in late afternoon. Came to a stop in the mountain road where two young men missed a curve, their car now visible under water in the river below us. They somehow had got ashore and climbed up the steep bank, a bank that was almost a cliff. A man in a camper, already carrying a logger with an injured hand to the hospital, took all three to Tofino. The empty yellow convertible, seeming to speed along under the river.

Thursday, August 4, 1977
Lantzville, Vancouver Island

Arbutus: those demonic trees that make every season autumn. I get
to rake leaves in the summer. Time, under arrest.

At low tide, on the beach, here: starfish, crabs, scallops, barnacles,
gulls, crows, one heron, a number of dogs barking at the gulls and
the crows and the one heron.

Received a card from Ron Smith. To me, in his house. Ron writing
from England, writing of John Ruskin:

Across the lake
the other side
of this century
Ruskin
        gone mad
landscaped a garden
the prospect from
that other side
admitting
            reluctantly
the season's torment

Friday, August 5, 1977
Lantzville, Vancouver Island

The book that was finished
isn't.

Out on one of the islands (nameless?) is a tiny structure that I for a
moment, when I arrived, took to be a lighthouse.

Suddenly, today, the men in the novel, in the middle of my
imaginary town that is not quite imaginary, in the middle of the
river that you could, possibly, if you insisted, visit — the men are
building a lighthouse. A lighthouse of blocks of perfect ice. They
make it taller. And then taller. They can't resist. They make it taller.

I tend the plants. I mow the grass. I feed the cats.

76

Saturday, August 6, 1977
Lantzville, Vancouver Island

Dinner last night in Nanaimo with Gladys Hindmarch and friends. Daphne Marlatt, those beautiful eyes streaming intelligence and love onto the mere world. Gladys herself transforming that world through her boat stories, her endlessly written and unwritten boat stories, her word-long telling of this coast. Against its silences. And Brian Fisher there too, too young for one so deep into the making of absolute forms. And Roy Kiyooka, that artist-poet who on dark days becomes for me a double, the wiseman I should have been; Roy from the prairies, ventured into rain forest, into the Basho-journeys of his far ancestors, into dream, into the color of words. We ate salmon and drank many bottles of wine.

Sunday, August 7, 1977
Lantzville, Vancouver Island

There's a crow in the book that talks, a crow identified by the men in the book, strangely enough, as the black crow. I noticed the crows here and began to talk to them, only briefly, only now and then; the neighbors didn't notice...and last night (Ron and Pat have a tantalizing collection of records, "Baroque Brass"...Purcell, Gabrielli, Bach, Holborne..."Virtuoso Music for Trumpet"...Paul Horn's record, "Inside"...I was listening, a small fire in the fireplace, partly to take off the chill, partly to give me an excuse to split some wood) — all of a sudden I spoke the title of the book. I heard myself say it: *What the Crow Said.*

There's an animal outside this house. It looks in the windows, at night. It comes up out of the water. Some nights it comes out of the water. Some nights it comes down out of the trees.

What are you frightened of? Nothing. What are you frightened of?

Wednesday, August 10, 1977
Lantzville, Vancouver Island

Went over on the ferry to Vancouver. Bought books at William Hoffer's bookstore — some scarce things by Daphne Marlatt. Hoffer, when I introduced myself, insisted he'd just read my first novel — and hated it. Then he felt better. Praised *The Studhorse Man.* Then I made the mistake of praising Eli Mandel's *Out of Place.* Hoffer fuming again. Then he felt better. Showed me the treasures of his bookstore. I read, loafed, browsed, met some of his friends when they dropped by. Hoffer, still, secretly, a Saskatchewan boy. Doing his thing on the West Coast....I went for a walk in Gastown. Had a meal in an East Indian restaurant. Back to the island on the CPR ferry. The harbor reminding me of Conrad. The Island, ahead of the ferry, its raised mountains set like blue teeth to the sun. I sat in the too-hot bar and tried to drink a beer. Went out on deck. Flirted briefly with a small young woman who was carrying a huge shoulder bag.

Saturday, August 13, 1977
Lantzville, Vancouver Island

Party tonight with John and Debbie Marshall. Their book-filled house right down on the beach. Met John years ago, under the stuffed animal heads in the Occidental Hotel. A beer with two undergraduates from Malaspina College, John Marshall and Steve Guppy. Ron Smith their teacher. Ron a publisher now, John and Steve a couple of the best young poets anywhere....John, now, serving drinks that kicked like a mule. We sat outside, lazy in the bright evening. Not a cloud in this West Coast sky since I arrived. Now, time to depart; I'll go away thinking of the coast as parched and rainless....We talk of young poets in the States. John, putting together another issue of his little magazine, *Island.* Debbie, talking of horses. Of the bookstore she's trying to start in Lantzville....Island people. Generous people. They ask about my book. I change the subject....

Saturday, September 10, 1977
Binghamton, New York

Back to teaching. I spend most of my waking hours in my office on campus. Rewriting some sections of the novel one last time. Preparing classes. Strange shifts in the graduate students in the two years since last I taught: a distrust of Modernism and its tenets. A graduate course in modern British literature. Doing some novels first, Hardy's *The Mayor of Casterbridge,* Conrad's *The Secret Agent*....A Fulbright student in the class, a young woman from Greece. Had to ask Bill Spanos how to pronounce her name....Heaps of manuscripts in the *boundary 2* office. Spanos at work on a special Creeley isue. I read poems and stories, some excellent work, knowing we have no room in the next few issues. What makes anyone become an editor?

Monday, October 17, 1977
Binghamton, New York

Smaro Kamboureli and I went for a drive, down to my favorite country tavern. Choconut. In rural Pennsylvania. Had a beer and listened to some country & western. Listened to the men at the bar telling hunting stories. Deer country. Drove then to Quaker Lake, through the rain. Ragged dairy farms with their tumbled old barns. Tree-hidden creeks and winding roads and sudden, small bridges. High, tree-crowned hills. This week, right now, the best time to see the color change in this hardwood eastern forest. Maple and oak. Red and yellow and brown. The trees that I've never quite learned to identify, for all my years here. Since 1961. When I arrived in the Susquehanna valley, in the maze of declining shoe-manufacturing towns. Smaro is excited to be here, studying contemporary American fiction, yet homesick for Greece, uneasy in this America with its strange customs, its blur of sounds. I have never been to Greece. She has never been to Canada. But maybe we are both strangers here, she, the visiting student, I, the familiar stranger.

Friday, April 28, 1978
Binghamton, New York

Ron Smith's story, "The Plimsoll Line," in the current issue of *The Malahat Review*. Risking its own pace, its own confrontation with stasis and motion. Two old people, island people, realized in fiction. Sitting in that Lantzville hotel where I sat and listened to some prairie people invent a ride back home.

I try to explain to Smaro that island. That Pacific shoreline. I try to explain, here in this Victorian house where I'm living now, this sabbatical house, as the expression has it — the owners in southern France until the end of July. Alex and Carol Fischler's spectacular three-story Victorian house, here in upstate New York. Gingerbread. Verandas. Two living rooms, one on either side of the entrance hall. High ceilings and an elegant staircase. The house itself an heirloom of a Binghamton that flourished in the last half of the 19th century. As the nation realized westward, leaving these houses behind, these cities behind. Smaro and I, studying, writing in the house. She in a room that overlooks a graveyard that has in it a perfect stone angel. I in a room, its windows screened by walnut trees. I've begun a poem about The Sad Phoenician of Love.

Thursday, May 18, 1978
Binghamton, New York

A letter today, from Julie Beddoes, the senior editor at General Publishing, thanking me for the hospitality. But she is the generous one, giving passionate support to my new manuscript. She flew down here from Toronto for two days. We sat for a whole day in the dining room, at the dining room table, surrounded by plants — turning the pages, discussing the text. The next day we finished in time to drive up to Cornell University, in Ithaca, to look at an ideal American university campus. SUNY-Binghamton is all newness, new buildings, for all the woods and fields of the old upstate farm that was transformed into a university. Cornell is towering spires and a huge quad and shade trees and stone buildings and statues and a spectacular series of waterfalls. A deep glen, leading down into the lake....Cayuga's waters....Julie's sense of the excitement, not so much of this, but of a new, bursting urban place like Toronto. My in-betweenness, my rural roots, my in fact having lived an urban life....Canadian universities tend to be in large cities. Cornell, finally, quaint to me. I like the new universities.

In a few weeks I leave here, move to the University of Manitoba.

Wednesday, June 14, 1978
Binghamton, New York

Meg's birthday today. Suddenly, 12. And so beautiful. Tall and
skinny, she is, at ease with the sun. She conned me into getting her a
10-speed bike, after we'd looked diligently at simpler models.

Today I finished correcting galleys. *What the Crow Said* is in air
freight, on its way back to Toronto. The book almost a book.
Scheduled for September. Book. Smaro and I had to rush to get
out to the airport before the flight left, then had difficulty finding
the air-freight office. I was driving back into town before I realized I
might never change another word in the story. That awful sense of
separation.

This evening, loafing, uneasy. I think about my talk with John
Gardner, the American novelist, when he was staying with Smaro
and me last week. Gardner, here, looking for a house. At night, our
talking about realism. Gardner, drinking into the night, conducting
his war with John Barth and Barth's kind of imagination, arguing
that you write out of what you "feel in your heart."

Saturday, June 24, 1978
Leduc, Alberta

I was in Edmonton yesterday as outside reader on a dissertation directed by Wilfred Watson, at the University of Alberta. Stayed overnight with the Harrisons. Breakfast with Dick and Irene this morning, in St. Albert. Bacon and eggs, coffee, toast made of bread that Irene baked from the wheat which she ground, wheat grown on the quarter-section that the Harrisons own and love, on the north bank of the North Saskatchewan, near Smokey Lake. Then back to bed. Then up again, and we loafed in the hot morning sun, the Harrisons' back yard a glory of trees and flowers. Irene is planning to grow roses this year. I read a little in Lorna Uher's new book of poems, *Crow's Black Joy*. A special book, handsomely printed by George Melnyk.

The Harrisons drove me to see Gary Geddes and his family, in Edmonton. Gary has taken a job in Montreal, he was packing. We drank a beer in the sun. Gary not at work on his Hong Kong poem.. He's doing a play for Paul Thompson right now. And starting a novel.

Al came into Edmonton for me in his pickup truck. Drove me out to Leduc. Al is hot-shotting these days — delivering special orders in Edmonton, or out to the oil rigs anywhere in the province. Kay is managing the new Dairy Queen in Leduc.

Pat and Harley have driven in from Vermilion. A birthday party for me. Lots of hockey talk. Young Pat McGill is succeeding as a player on the west coast. Comic stories of the violence of the audience, not the players. Cousin Lorne out from the city. Drinking a bit, the men. And swapping stories in a way that once again makes me realize where the method of *What the Crow Said* really comes from. I listen.

A wonderful huge supper. A cake with 51 candles. I blew them all out at one try.

Saturday, July 8, 1978
Binghamton, New York

Mail this afternoon: a Xeroxed copy of the dust jacket of *Crow*. An
exciting cover. Smaro delighted, insisting on holding it when I put it
on another book to see what it would look like. We couldn't work,
went for a drive to buy some silver forks and spoons in Stedman's
Junkshop, in the town of Union; went to Lescron's, a huge
secondhand bookstore, to ask Gil Williams about books on the
Phoenicians. Ended up with a copy of *Settlers In Canada*, a lovely
old edition.

Smaro giving me ideas about how to use the idea of color in the Sad
Phoenician poems; colors becoming voices, becoming characters;
the dialectic of hearing and seeing.

Steak and corn on the cob. Put out the cobs for the raccoon that
seems to live now somewhere in the maze of flowers and trees and
berry bushes in our back yard.

Friday, July 21, 1978
Binghamton, New York

Today I moved out of my SUNY-Binghamton office, took out my typewriter and a last box of notes and turned in the keys. Arrived here almost 17 years ago. Seventeen years next month, as I recollect: driving into town from Iowa City with all my possessions, except for some boxes of books that I mailed, in the car. And all my own books published during my stay here. Beginning with *But We Are Exiles.*

And what is exile?

Read Patty Daneman's short story, my last official "duty." Returned it to her this morning. Three students with Incompletes. But I've yet to see their papers. Many letters of recommendation still to write, no doubt. And some editing for *boundary 2.*

Binghamton. My daughters, Meg and Laura, born here. Staying here with their mother. Home. Perhaps my father, born in Ontario, growing up in Ontario, felt he was an exile in Alberta.

Smaro. From Greece. Bored tonight in Binghamton. Rain and heat at once, tonight. Smaro full of memories. And sad.

Repaired the oak desk that we bought for Smaro in a junk shop in Owego. Fixed a crack in my wooden chair, the chair I used for years in my office. I bought it in the Volunteers of America store. Here in Binghamton. I bought two chairs; the other one is in the basement of the house on Lathrop Avenue, where I lived.

A LIST OF NAMES OF PEOPLE CLOSE TO KROETSCH

January 22, 1974:   Margaret (Meg) & Laura Kroetsch: his daughters.

March 9, 1974: Sheila Medeiros: his sister; Lee Medeiros: her husband.

August 21, 1974: William Spanos: co-editor, with Kroetsch, of *boundary 2*.

June 24, 1978: Kay McGill: his sister; Al: her husband; Pat Youngberg: his sister; Harley: her husband.

Smaro in front of the house on Riverside Drive, Binghamton

Rudy Wiebe

Andrew Suknaski in 1979   *photo by Peter Sutherland*

photo by Ron Smith

Robert Kroetsch in Cathedral Grove, Vancouver Island

Credits:
Editor: Douglas Barbour
Publisher: George Melnyk
Assistant Publisher: Jack Lewis
Cover Design: Alan Brownoff
Typesetting: Bev Ruhl
Layout: Don McIntosh
Printing: Willis Printing and Lithography Co. Ltd. and Stuart Brandle Printing Services Ltd.
Binding: Tri-Tradesman Bindery Ltd. and Universal Bindery Ltd.
Financial Assistance: Alberta Culture

Published with the financial assistance
of the Canada Council.